Finding Autumn Bliss

Dan Weaver-White
Foreword By Jacob Coy

Finding Autumn Bliss

ISBN 978-1-7331489-0-0

Author & Photographer: Dan Weaver-White
Foreword: Jacob Coy
Copy Editor: Jeff Weaver-White

That the generation to come might know them, even the children which should be born;
who should arise and declare them to their children. Psalms 78:6

Dedication

I have been blessed to know so many strong women who have faced the challenges of life with strength, determination, and a willingness to pattern the direction of their lives after the sunflower, which always follows the brightness and warmth of the sun. I dedicate this book to them.

Ruth Cutsinger

Stacee Droit

Pauletta Hammers

Jerrah Henson

Jamie Hertter

Olive Hinckle-Sparks

Diane Nadaf

Darlene Weaver

Thank you for bringing peace to my heart!

Table of Contents

Foreword

The blissful season of autumn is upon us once again. It is a special time filled with magic and beauty. Leaves are beginning to change and show signs of color, pumpkins are ready to be harvested, apples are ready to be picked, and a cool chill is in the air as the days become shorter and nights become longer. There is so much simple autumn beauty at work. Autumn is also a time of peace and comfort. With so much change happening all around, it's a time to reminisce and think back on simpler times.

My name is Jake, and I have a deep-rooted love for the past. Ever since I was a child, I can remember being surrounded by early antiques. I was fascinated by tavern tables, pewter chargers, painted blanket chests, and comb-back rocking chairs. The creaking sound of the old rocking chairs and the worn table tops were the most wonderful things. The most influential part of my childhood was not only being around early antiques, but being around the women who housed them and held the stories of their origins. My grandmother, or as I called her, Muzzie, taught me everything I know about antiques, family history, gardening, and crafting.

I loved going over to Muzzie's old house, sitting in her comb-back rocker, and simply listening to her talk about her upbringing in Vermont and our family roots there. She'd tell me the story about the tavern table carried by horseback from New Jersey to Vermont, and how the early Pennsylvanian Dutch blanket chest was painted by my great, great grandmother. The majority of Muzzie's collection came from her family: antiques passed down from generation to generation. She later taught me about decorating with primitive antiques and introduced me to many antique shows. She helped me build my collection, guided me to buy what I love, and even helped me start my own antique business. Even though Muzzie is no longer with me in the physical sense, the lessons, stories, and love for antiques she instilled in me will always be a part of who I am.

It has brought me such bliss becoming an avid collector and dealer. Though I'm just embarking on this journey, I've learned that becoming an antique dealer is a process just like accumulating a great collection. I started out by making dried goods from my garden, such as bean garlands, gourd clusters, and herb wreaths. I would use the money I made to buy antiques for my personal collection. I later used my earnings to buy antiques to resell. I began to acquire more antiques and blend them with my dried naturals while doing more shows. To this day, I still blend those two elements as I continue collecting and dealing. I am beyond excited to continue on, learn, and explore this industry.

As I've continued collecting, selling, crafting, and creating, I've made some wonderful friends along the way. Dan and Jeff are among those close friends I've come to know over the years. Dan and I both have a passion for the past, but we share something so much greater than just collecting antiques. We may live in different states and we may be different ages, but we both know what it's like to have such a strong, incredible, influential grandmother. Dan's grandmother, Ruth Cutsinger, taught him many lessons and encouraged him to believe in the impossible. Ruth was easily Dan's greatest mentor, as Muzzie was my greatest mentor. Dan and I both know what it's like to have a person in our lives fuel our passions, even after they are no longer physically here with us. We go forward with the knowledge and bliss that two incredibly valuable women were once here and will always inspire us.

As you read *Finding Autumn Bliss*, you too will be reminded of those influential people in your life. Throughout these blissful pages, you will see how one person influenced and inspired another's life. Dan has poured so much of his emotions and experiences into writing *Finding Autumn Bliss*, and I know you will love and enjoy every page of it. As the autumn breeze blows and the leaves fall down, enjoy your visit at Peace Manor!

All My Best,

Jacob Matthew Coy

Jake's Cabin Primitives

Introduction

During the autumn of 2014, I was in the deepest, darkest pit of my life. It seemed I had lost all of my faith and that my life had unraveled to a point that I no longer recognized it. In many ways, the life I had once known was dead and gone, and I was left wondering which direction to turn. Finding bliss during that autumn was the furthest thing from my mind. Even simply finding the strength to put one foot in front of the other seemed almost insurmountable. As the days began to get shorter and the nights grew much cooler, I realized that my life had begun to unravel almost exactly one year earlier on my 41st birthday, which was on November 2nd. A year had passed, and my birthday was quickly approaching once again. On the last night of my 41st year, I laid in bed hoping that the next year would be better and that I would find the answers that I sought, but most of all I hoped that I would be able to climb my way out of the pit that had all but swallowed me whole. My prayer that night was for peace, something that I was desperately trying to find. As I began to fall asleep, I could have never imagined what was in store for me.

In the early hours of November 2nd, 2014, I had a dream. I saw before my eyes a saltbox house. It had dark gray siding and striking red windows. Even now, I remember how I felt gazing at the house in my dreams. There was a sense of peace that enveloped me, and I felt happy for the first time in a very long time. When I awoke from my dream I literally said out loud, "Oh, that's right. I used to want to live in a saltbox." How could I have forgotten that? I had dreamed of living in a saltbox house since first seeing one in *County Living* magazine 11 years earlier, but still I had forgotten. As I laid in bed and remembered my dream of living in a saltbox house, I began to feel like I had while dreaming a few moments earlier, and in that very moment, I took my first step up out of my pit.

Some would say, "It is just a house," but to me it was one of the first rungs on the ladder that helped me climb my way out of the dark pit that I had found myself in that autumn. So when I have said over and over that the house featured in this book is a miracle, I mean that quite literally. In many ways this house was part of the new life that Jeff and I carved out for ourselves. The road to finding the bliss and peace that I so longed for that last night of my 41st year has been paved with many bumps and detours, but it has also been filled with many joys and celebrations.

As you begin your journey into this book that has been dedicated to the season of autumn, I also want you to see another theme that is very important to me. I want you to see that even when everything seems lost, something new can be found. I want you to read about seemingly impossible miracles, and I want you to read heartwarming stories of love and strength. I want you fully to understand what my grandma, Ruth Cutsinger, meant when she repeatedly told me, "God can make a way where there seems to be no way." This book and the house featured in its pages are a result of God making a way where there seemed to be no way. It is also my hope that as you make your way through this book you will be reminded of another lesson my grandma always taught me. She never missed an opportunity to remind me that "faith, even the size of a mustard seed, could move mountains." The dream I had on the morning of my 42nd birthday, be it small like the mustard seed, was just enough faith to begin to move the mountain that stood before me.

All of our lives are a tapestry of experiences and encounters. We learn something from every single experience that comes our way. Everything that happens to us is meant for us and is placed in our path to make us better people. The trials of this life are not meant to make us bitter; they are meant to make us better. Hard times befall all of us, but they are not punishments. They are actually blessings because of the lessons they teach us. I know that some of you reading this right now may be in a deep, dark pit. I know that some of you may be staring at an enormous mountain wondering how it will ever move. My advice to you is to not give up, to take one day at a time and to remember that God will supply the rungs that you will need to climb your way out of your pit. Each rung will come to you at precisely the right time because, like my grandma always said, "God's timing is perfect." Never lose hope and continue to walk the path that has been laid before you. It will inevitably lead you to the place where you were intended to arrive.

Bliss is defined as perfect happiness or great joy, and I hope that when you get to the last page of this book that is what you feel. However, even more than bliss, I hope you feel encouraged. I hope you feel inspired, and I hope you feel ready to tackle any problem that may come your way. I hope you find yourself believing more in miracles, and I hope you understand the importance of believing in those miracles and in telling the story of your life. We all have stories to tell, and each story is meant to be told and is meant to encourage others. To me, finding inspiration and encouragement while looking at pictures of a house decorated in the early/primitive style is the best of both worlds, and my sincere hope is that when you are finished reading this book, you will agree with me. Autumn is the time of year that we harvest what we have sown. My wish for all of you is that you reap the benefits of the determination, love, laughter, and faith that you have sown in your lives and that when you see the first autumn leaf turn a crimson red or a brilliant yellow that you will feel peace and you will begin the joyous journey to *Finding Autumn Bliss.*

All My Best,

Dan Weaver White

Foyer

ce the foyer is the first space that guests see when entering our house, I wanted to do something unique
d unexpected when decorating it for autumn. Jeff and I always line the outside steps that lead to the front
or with large, orange pumpkins, so I thought it would be interesting to repeat the look on the steps that
d to the second story of the house. The end result was so much better than I could have imagined. The
mpkins added a pop of color and made the foyer feel a little bit like a pumpkin patch. Smaller pumpkins
re added to the blue bench in the entry hall, along with a black cat and a scarecrow from Arnett's Country
re. The entire space had a very welcoming autumnal feeling that was warm and inviting.

ABOVE: A scarecrow, which was made by Stacee Droit of Arnett's County Store, is tucked into an early tobacco basket. The basket is attached to the wall and sits on an early blue bench. The early barn lantern, hogscraper candlesticks, basket, and a remnant of an early Oriental rug finish off the display.

LEFT: For an unexpected and natural look, fresh pumpkins have been placed on each step of the stairway in the foyer.

OPPOSITE: To fill a large space on the wall in the foyer, an early log cabin quilt has been hung using small tacks. The quilt fills in the space nicely, while adding color and warmth.

If I Had a Remembrance Book

Anyone who knows me has heard many stories about my grandma and about the miracles that were performed in her life. However, what most people do not know is long before I was able to reach people with stories of my grandma's life, she was telling the stories of her life and of the miracles that God had performed for her mother, Olive Hinckle-Sparks. My grandma felt it was her calling and her mission in life to make sure that all of the miracles that God performed for her mother would not be forgotten and would live on long after her mom had gone to heaven. One story that my grandma loved to tell was about a time during the depression when her family did not have anything to eat and how God supplied their needs. The following is that story taken from my grandma's writings, a recorded testimonial that she gave at church, and stories that she had told me over the years.

If I had a remembrance book, I would write about a time when I was a little girl and my family did not have anything to eat. In fact, as my mom would have said, there was not even a dust of flour in the house. I remember a morning very many years ago when I was lying in my bed and I heard my mom's voice coming from behind the heating stove. Her voice was really low and soft, and she was praying. I can remember her prayer just like it was yesterday. She said, "Lord you know that I have children who have to get up pretty soon and go to school. I don't even have a dust of flour in this house to fix them any breakfast. You promised to supply our needs." All of a sudden my mom got really quiet and I thought, "Well, she is going to go back to bed." However, the next thing I heard were the lids on the stove being lifted up. She was going to build a fire in the cook stove.

My dad woke up about that time, and I heard him say, "Olive, what are you doing?" My mom replied, "I'm going to build a fire. There is going to be food here in just a little while for me to cook for these children." When my dad heard this, he gruffly said, "You are crazy! There is not any food to eat in this house, and it is 6:00 in the morning. There is not going to be any food brought into this house." My mom was not deterred. She simply stated, "Nevertheless, the Lord has spoken to me, and He has assured me that there is going to be food in this house, and I believe there will be food."

Meanwhile, unbeknownst to us, Brother Newton was across town in his barn milking his cows. He later told us that the Lord spoke to him in his barn that morning and said, "Brother and Sister Hinckle's family is in dire need of food this morning. I want you to take them some food." He said that he excitedly made his way to the house to tell his wife what had happened. When he walked into the kitchen, he told his wife, Sister Newton, about what the Lord had told him to do. She looked at him with amazement and said, "The Lord has already spoken to me, too. I have already begun gathering up food for them." Well, you can imagine what Brother and Sister Newton must have felt that morning. They were about to perform a miracle for us, but at the same time, they could not help but know that God speaking to both of them at the same time was a miracle in and of itself. In fact, Brother Newton later told us that Sister Newton shouted praises to the Lord every time she made a trip from the house to the car with another load of food.

At about 6:30 a.m. there was a knock on our front door. When my mom answered the door, there stood

Brother Newton. He said, "Sister Hinkle, I do not know what you are going to think of this, but I have a carload of food that I brought for you this morning. You could almost feel the wave of relief and praise that flowed through that house in that moment as my mom said, "Well, Brother Newton, just come on in! The Lord has already told me that someone was coming with food." Even now, all these years later, I can still see that great big table filling up with food. There was a slab of bacon, sweet potatoes, Irish potatoes, and a ham. There was even a cracker box full of hot biscuits that Sister Newton had baked for her family, but she gave them to us so that we could have warm biscuits that morning. There was enough food brought that morning to last at least two or three months. It seems like in my mind that it may have lasted six months.

That is just one of the many miracles that God performed for my mom and our family. It was during the time of the depression, and people had to depend on God to answer our prayers. Even though the depression is over, we should all still depend on God to answer our prayers. Even all these years later, God is still in the miracle-making, prayer-answering business, and I am so thankful for that. It is like my mom always taught me, God can make a way where there seems to be no way, and the Lord will never leave us or forsake us. I am so thankful to have learned those lessons firsthand.

Living Room

Even though the living room is somewhat formal, I wanted to give it a casual, autumnal feeling by includir a few natural pumpkins. I lined the mantel of the fireplace with small orange pumpkins and added a single white pumpkin into the display that tops the early red apothecary cabinet. I placed additional pumpkins o the slant top desk and on the trunk behind the sofa. I placed a white pumpkin with a long, misshapen stem on the game table that sits in front of the fireplace. I added some folk art to the room by including a witch and a black cat made by Stacee Droit and a Halloween sampler made by Bridgett Swindle. The living roor maintained its formal feel but still allowed the fun of the season to be highlighted.

ABOVE: An early apothecary cabinet with original red paint occupies the center of a long wall in the living room. An apothecary cabinet gets its name from a druggist's cabinet from days gone by, which had many drawers for keeping medicines, herbs, and spices separated. LEFT: Two early rye baskets sit atop the apothecary cabinet. An early oil painting hangs above the cabinet to give the display added height.

ABOVE: An early slant top desk with its original red paint is positioned in the corner of the living room. The early stool provides a place to sit and "figure." RIGHT: A pile of tiny early leather books sits on the desk next to a tiny pumpkin. The small hooked rug, which was made by Betty Zahn, appears centuries older than it actually is and adds softness and color to the desk.

An Early Green Firkin

If I were asked to list my favorite collections, I do not think it would come as a surprise to anyone to find out that firkins would top the list. Firkins, also called sugar buckets, were once used to store items like grain, sugar, and flour. Because many firkins date back to colonial times, I am always amazed by how many have survived. When I was first beginning to decorate in the primitive style, I used to dream of owning just one early firkin. To be honest, I never thought my dream would come true, but like many dreams it did come true, and now I own more firkins than I ever imagined was possible. As you may have noticed, I am a huge fan of color, so my collection of firkins represents a rainbow of early colors.

I am often asked which firkin is my favorite, or which color is my favorite, or if I store anything in my firkins. I usually answer these questions very quickly and always say that I do not store anything in my firkins. I guess this has been a small mistruth, but I think when you hear my story you will understand why I have answered as I have.

In the autumn of 2006, Jeff and I made a decision that would change our lives and our hearts forever; we decided to become parents. We did not want to become parents in the traditional sense, so we became parents to a beautiful, be it a bit hyper, miniature schnauzer who we named Parker McKenzie, Parker after Sarah Jessica Parker and McKenzie after the family's last name in the movie *Peyton Place*. Parker was the perfect girl! She was loving, obedient, and smart. Parker never really knew she was a dog, and my mother-in-law always referred to her the perfect lady, and she truly was.

We loved Parker so much and she brought us so much joy that in the summer of 2007 we decided to become parents again. This time were blessed with a bundle of pure, unadulterated joy and love all embodied in a snow-white miniature schnauzer named Peyton McEntire. Peyton was all boy. He got his name from the movie *Peyton Place* and from one of my favorite singers, Reba McEntire. Peyton was happy every single day of his life. He awoke each morning with a smile on his face, and his whole entire body wiggled with love and excitement. Peyton never met a stranger and was a protector of his pack, and his pack stretched further than the house in which he lived.

The four of us were all very happy, and then in the winter of 2009, the baby bug hit Jeff again, and this time we adopted a black miniature schnauzer who was pure evil. I never thought a cute little girl could be so mean, but she truly was. Her name was Paycee McLaine. Paycee was named after a character from the television show *Dawson's Creek* and the actress Shirley MacLaine. Paycee was into everything, and she destroyed anything she could get her paws or her teeth on. Some of you may remember our three miniature schnauzers because I called them the Ps x 3. I thought we were crazy for having three dogs, and there were times when I honestly thought that I couldn't possibly continue with the insanity. Miraculously, one morning Paycee woke up and decided to become the most perfect dog that God ever created. It was like a switch was flipped in her. She went from pure evil to absolute perfection literally overnight. We now had the perfect family. All three dogs were special in their own way, and the five of us were very happy.

adly in March of 2015, Parker was diagnosed with cancer and died within just few days. The sudden and arring loss of Parker took us completely by surprise. She was only eight years old. How could she be gone? t was difficult to understand, but when we returned from the hospital where Parker had passed away, we were greeted by Peyton and Paycee and, even though we were extremely sad, their excitement to see us nd their love for us softened the blow of Parker's death. In time, our hearts mended, and we were all once gain very happy.

n January of 2017, Peyton became ill, so we took him to see his doctor, and she told us that he had liver ancer and that he would more than likely never return home. We were once again devastated and could ot imagine losing Peyton, but God wasn't finished with him yet. He decided to heal our boy. His doctor ame up with a treatment plan, and it worked better than anyone could have ever hoped. It was not an nstant healing, but even Peyton's doctor stated that she could not understand why Peyton continued to ve and said that he was indeed a miracle. He went from multiple organ failure and taking several nedications everyday to completely normal organ function, and he eventually stopped taking medication ltogether. Peyton's life was spared, and there was not a day that went by that we did not thank God for iving us one more day with him.

n November of 2019, we realized that our boy was once again suffering. We tried many different things vith the help of Peyton's doctor, but in the end we all realized that his time had run out. The day after Christmas, Jeff, Paycee, and I encircled our little miracle with love and watched him peacefully pass away. n last few moments of his life, Peyton was surrounded by love and by his pack. I know he was very pleased, and I know that he was reunited with Parker that day and that they will live on forever in the nost beautiful place that any of us can ever imagine. I also know that Jeff and I will be reunited with hem one day and that Paycee will eventually see them again as well.

As crazy as I thought we were for having three dogs, I know that God's plan was perfect. He knew that Parker's life would be cut short, and he knew that Peyton would need a companion. He also knew that we eeded a dog to help us with the loss of Peyton. That evil little girl turned perfect angel has been by our ide since her brother has gone to heaven, and we sure are thankful for her!

Parker and Peyton were both cremated, and when the little boxes that contained their remains were eturned to us, I placed them in an early green firkin, and that is where they will stay until Jeff and I make our journey to see them again. So you see, I never thought I would own an early firkin, much less have a ollection of them, but now one of them holds two very special angels that have changed our lives and I ike to think maybe even the world in some ways. We can all learn so much from dogs. They love unconditionally, they see the good in everyone, and they greet everyday with excitement and wonder. All hey want is to love and to be loved by their pack, and they never judge anyone at all. Love is all that is mportant to a dog.

o now whenever someone asks me which firkin is my favorite or if I store anything in my firkins, I very proudly point to an early green firkin and say, "I store love, laughter, loyalty, and a couple of pieces of my eart in that early green firkin." Having a dog in our lives and seeing the world through their eyes can pring so much peace to our lives, and *PEACE MATTERS*.

Dining Room

Even though we do not use the dining room often, it is my favorite room in the house. I love the coziness of this space and its wood walls and ceilings. The dining room is also one of the most colorful rooms in the house. The early firkins and pantry boxes in varying colors add so much warmth and color to the room. During the autumn, I like to continue the color theme by adding lots of natural pumpkins and gourds of differing sizes and colors. In the middle of the dining room table, which is an early round table with its original blue legs, I wanted to create an unexpected centerpiece. The table has a built-in Lazy Susan, so I decided to place a large orange pumpkin in an oversized, shallow rye basket and then surround the pumpkin with small, colorful gourds. The final result was exactly what I wanted it to be. The rest of the room is filled with orange and white pumpkins, which make the entire room feel cohesive and ready for a family meal.

LEFT: An early cupboard with original mustard paint hangs above an early blue grain bin in the corner of the dining room.

RIGHT: In the opposite corner of the dining room is an early wall table that has been lowered to provide additional display space.

LEFT: An early corner cupboard is situated next to an early drying rack, which has early blue homespun hanging from it. Above the drying rack hangs a small early sampler.

RIGHT: Early salt-glazed crock jugs with cobalt blue designs occupy the shelves of the corner cupboard. Small white pumpkins have been added to the shelves to provide a touch of autumn.

ABOVE: An early slant top desk hangs under a pumpkin-colored shelf near the window in the dining room. The black pumpkin head with witch hat was made by Stacee Droit of Arnett's Country Store. OPPOSITE: The focal point in the dining room is an early red bucket shelf that has been filled with a collection of early firkins and pantry boxes in their original, vibrant colors. Small bright-orange pumpkins have been displayed on the shelves to celebrate the season.

Finding Autumn Bliss

LEFT: The top of an early blue grain bin has been filled with two early measures and a piggin, which is an oversized scoop used during colonial times to scatter grain for chickens, to slop the hogs, or as a one-handled milk bucket. The round breadboard is the perfect place to display an early scoop and reproduction tin light.

RIGHT: An early red dry sink has been filled with two early bowls, an orange pumpkin with a long stem, and a tin light.

You Gotta Show Love

As humans, we are capable of many different emotions. We can be sad, we can be mad, we can feel envy, we can feel guilt, and most importantly, we can feel love. To me, the greatest of all of human emotions is the ability to show love. We learn how to express our emotions as children. How many of us have said, "I am a worrier, just like my mom," or "When I get mad, you can see it all over my face. My dad was the same way"? We learn how to express our emotions at a very early age, and those lessons stay with us until the end of our lives. As children, we watch the people around us. We listen to them and we emulate them, whether we want to or not. The Bible says that we should have hope, faith, and love and then adds that the greatest of these is love. In First Corinthians, several verses are dedicated to the characteristics of love. There are millions of songs dedicated to love. There are entire movies that are centered on love, and there are entire books written about finding love. That is how important love is. Love truly does make the world go round.

On an autumn day in 1925, my grandma, Ruth Cutsinger, was born. She lived on this earth for ninety years, and in that time, love was the message that she chose to speak of and teach. My grandma had no trouble showing love. She was never backwards about telling people that she loved them, even if she did not know them very well. When my grandma died, everyone told stories about how she showed love to them or someone they knew. Love was always the answer to every problem that my grandma faced in life. It may have taken her a while to come to that conclusion, but inevitably she would find her way back to the same answer, "You gotta show love." If I heard her say that once, I probably heard her say it a thousand times. In so many ways, it was her anthem, her theme song, and her catchphrase, and now that she is gone, her words continue to echo in my mind and in the minds of all who knew her. Even now, all of the people who loved her will remind each other, "You know, you gotta show love." How proud my grandma would be to know that her words have outlived her. Her words have an immortality of sorts.

There are so many ways to show love, and I implore you to find a way to show love to someone every single day of your life. It can be anyone. It can be a stranger, a friend, or a family member. Do something everyday to show love, and when you do it, think of someone like my grandma who taught you the importance of showing love. I truly cannot think of a better way to honor the people who have loved us than to show love in their memory.

Love is what will change this world. Fighting and yelling and making accusations will not make the world a better place. Only love can do that. Never forget that children are watching all of us, and they are learning how to express their emotions by observing how we express ours. I think if we all remember that a little more, we may stop ourselves from showing emotions that are not borne from love. Maybe we all should say to ourselves more often, "You know, you gotta show love." Showing love and expressing love will bring peace to our lives and to the entire world, and *PEACE MATTERS*!

PEACE MANOR

Kitchen

The kitchen is one of the biggest rooms in our house, so it can be a challenge to make it feel cozy and famil[y] friendly. However, during the autumn I am able to make it feel even more like the heart of the home by adding fresh pumpkins and other fall produce to the space. When autumn begins to dot the landscape outside the three windows over the soapstone farmhouse sink, I begin to fill wooden bowls with a variety o[f] apples. I also place large pumpkins in other wooden bowls and display pumpkins on breadboards and countertops. I also display a collection of small pumpkins on the windowsill, which makes the windows fee[l] even more special. The kitchen is the place where we spend most of our time, so it is important that the sights and scents of autumn fill the room throughout the season.

LEFT: The shelves of a cabinet, which was inspired by the kitchen in the television show *Downton Abbey*, hold a collection of early redware and tool caddies. Early apothecary jars and wooden mashers are also displayed on the countertop.

RIGHT: An early dough box sits in the center of the kitchen island, while an early breadboard serves as an additional space to prepare food. The countertops in the kitchen are maple.

ABOVE: The Windsor-style barstools were made by Benner's Woodworking, which is located in Lebanon, Ohio. An early Oriental rug has been placed in front of the oven to give the kitchen an earlier feel.
LEFT: A large pumpkin has been placed in an oversized early wooden bowl to add color and an autumnal feeling to the kitchen.

ABOVE: An early harvest table with its original blue apron and legs sits in the center of the keeping room. Reproduction Windsor chairs surround the table. The table and chairs sit on a vintage braided rug. For the autumn, the wooden bowls on the table have been filled with a pumpkin and red and green apples. RIGHT: The Peace Manor sign, which was made by George and Darlene Weaver, hangs above the soapstone farmhouse-style sink.

Pumpkin Pie Cake

Anyone who knew my grandma, Ruth Cutsinger, would say that one of her greatest joys in life was baking. It is something that she did almost everyday of her life. Her cakes and pies were legendary, and even now people continue to reminisce about them. Each person in my grandma's life had a favorite cake or pie, and she made that cake or pie every year on their birthday. Since my birthday is in the autumn, my favorite was my grandmas's pumpkin pie cake. She loved to make the cake for me each year, and it was always a big hit at my party. Baking for others truly fed my grandma's spirit. It gave her a sense of accomplishment, and she loved for people to brag on her baked goods. Since this book is all about autumn, I thought it would be a great recipe to share with you. I know it would thrill my grandma if you would make this cake and share it with your friends and family. And when you do, I hope that you think of my grandma and the life she led, and I hope it will bring you peace because **PEACE MATTERS**.

Pumpkin Pie Cake

C flour	2 C sugar
/2 TB salt	4 eggs
TB cinnamon	1 C oil
TB baking soda	2 C pumpkin
TB baking powder	1 C chopped pecans

Mix, four, salt, cinnamon, baking soda, and baking powder together. In another bowl, mix eggs, oil, and sugar together. Add dry ingredients, pumpkin, and pecans and mix well. Pour batter into two greased and floured 9 inch cake pans. Bake at 350 degrees for 30-40 minutes.

Frosting

pkg. Dream Whip
oz softened cream cheese
C milk
box Betty Crocker Home-
Style Fluffy White Frosting Mix

Combine Dream Whip and milk and beat until icing is stiff. In another bowl, beat the softened cream cheese until it is creamy. Combine the Dream Whip and cream cheese and pour in the Fluffy White mix and then beat until the icing is smooth. Apply icing to the well-cooled cake and garnish with chopped pecans.

Keeping Room

The keeping room, which was sometimes referred to as the hearth room during colonial times, is another space that Jeff, Paycee, and I use on a daily basis. I recently was able to place two sofas in the keeping room facing each other in front of the fireplace. This simple furniture rearrangement transformed the keeping room into a more comfortable space and makes it a favorite place for company to gather. During autumn, like to fill the space with pumpkins of different sizes and colors. I like to tuck the pumpkins into unexpected spaces and allow them to become a sort of art form in the room. I also like to use gourds and seasonal folk art made by my friend, Stacee Droit of Arnett's County Store. During the cool autumn evenings, the keeping room is filled with love, laughter and a very sweet, sleeping miniature schnauzer.

LEFT: An early pie safe that dates back to the mid 19th century retains its original green and red paint. An early rocking horse sits atop the pie safe. An early hooked rug with a geometric pattern adds warmth to the area and serves as the perfect accent.

RIGHT: An early dough box on legs serves as a coffee table between the two sofas in the keeping room. The top of the dough box is easily removed, allowing the box to be used as storage for blankets and pillows.

ABOVE: The shelves of an early stepback cupboard are the ideal place to display a collection of early pantry boxes in varying colors and sizes. The variety of colors of pantry boxes allows collectors of early antiques to add color to their homes, while still remaining true to their love of the time period. RIGHT: An Arnett's Country Store scarecrow with an orange pumpkin head stands in front of the open shelves of the stepback.

Finding Autumn Bliss

LEFT: An early blue plate rack showcases a collection of early treen plates. An early sampler hangs above the plate rack. BELOW LEFT: An early hooked rug provides a soft backdrop for an early horse with original white paint. BELOW: An early sampler is displayed on the door of an early blue hanging cupboard.

ABOVE: An early pie rack, which was once used to cool pies, has been hung on the fireplace surround in the keeping room and is now used as a make-do drying rack. Several remnants of early blue calico hang from the "drying rack." The three early samplers above the fireplace were made by a trio of sisters in the 19th century. RIGHT: Two tin Revere lanterns hang from the mantel.

OPPOSITE: A stack of early trucks, each with original paint, sits under an early drain board that has been displayed on the wall. The early black Windsor chair in front of the window is the perfect perch for a black cat made by Stacee Droit and a white pumpkin. LEFT: A make-do dry sink has been created by placing an early breadboard on top of an early red bin.

RIGHT: A narrow early bench has been placed in front of the window and topped with three pumpkins.

OPPOSITE: All of the tin chandeliers were handmade by Carriage House Lighting, which is located in Troy, Ohio.

ABOVE: A large piece of early linen has been fashioned into a table runner and placed on the early harvest table in the keeping room.

A Thankful Heart

As we all busily prepare for Thanksgiving each year, we find ourselves using words like thankful and grateful. They flow out of our mouths with such ease that it seems that we use them every single day. There is something about preparing the biggest meal of the year and gathering with our friends and families that puts the words thankful and grateful at the forefront of our thoughts. When we gather together on Thanksgiving, many of us relay to others all of the blessings that we have in our lives. We go around the table and each person recites his list of things for which he is thankful. In school, we encourage our students to tell us what they are thankful for, and in our churches we sing songs and give testimonials about all of the blessings that we have received from God. We seem to think that it would not be Thanksgiving if we did not go through this yearly ritual.

Being thankful on Thanksgiving is a hugely important thing to do, but often once the turkey is eaten, the pumpkin pie has been sliced, and the dishes are washed, we are no longer as thankful as we know we should be. It is not that we do not have anything to be thankful for, but the ordinariness of our lives and the negative things of the world quickly begin to weigh us down again, and we find ourselves focusing more on the negative things associated with life than the positive things.

Having a thankful heart and being grateful for all that we have should not be something that we do once or twice a year. It should be a way of life for all of us. When we have a grateful heart, we have more peace in our lives. When we have a grateful heart, we have less negativity in our lives, and we see events and situations in a different light. When we live our lives with a thankful heart, we feel lighter and happier. We feel that life does have meaning and that we can overcome all of the obstacles that come our way.

I know that in my own life there have been times when it was a struggle for me to think of something that I was grateful for, but looking back on the valleys of my life now, I can see that there certainly were always many things to be grateful for. If the valleys of life do nothing more for us, they teach us just how much we have to be thankful for. Of course the valleys of life teach us far more than that. They teach us to have faith, to be strong, and to lean on God. They show us that God is still in the miracle-making, prayer-answering business, and we eventually realize that had we not walked through the valley we would not have all the blessings that we now have.

I, like most people, become very reflective during this time of year, and I have increasingly found myself being thankful for the valleys in my life. When we gather on Thanksgiving, we find ourselves being thankful for the same things year after year. The things that we list are so very important, and they certainly are blessings that we should be thankful for, but maybe we should also try to reflect on the things that we did not think were blessings when they first occurred.

Maybe we should say that we are thankful for the valleys and turbulent times in our lives as well. Maybe we should say that we are thankful for the pain that we endured this year, whether it was physical, mental or emotional. Maybe we should list the times we have been disheartened or depressed. I believe that if we all would do this, we would see just how far we have come because of those trials. I believe we would see much God was with us during those times, and I believe that other people will begin to see their own ...ggles in very different ways. When they see that we can actually be thankful for the valleys in our own ..., they will begin to see the valleys of their lives differently.

...have all been called to bring light to the world. We have all been called to show what miracles God is ...able of doing, and sharing our struggles and being truly thankful for them is one of the many ways that ...can answer our calling. Being thankful for the struggles in this life and realizing that with God's help we ...overcome those struggles and be better, stronger people because of them will help all of us live ...ryday with a grateful heart. We will find ourselves sharing what we are grateful for, not just on ...nksgiving Day, but every day that we live. Being grateful and truly living with an attitude of ...nkfulness will lead to peace, and *PEACE MATTERS*.

Breakfast Room

Breakfast room, breakfast room, how do I love thee? Let me count the ways. There are so many reasons why I love our little breakfast room. I love it for its five large, divided windows that let in so much light and provide spectacular views of the country landscape that surrounds our saltbox. I love it for its wood walls and floors and for its soaring ten-foot-high wooden ceiling. The breakfast room is the first room one sees when entering the back door, and it always brings a smile to my face. During the autumn, I fill the breakfast room with lots of pumpkins, and I created a centerpiece on the early sawbuck table by filling a large wooden bowl with lots of small pie pumpkins. The breakfast room is also the place that Jeff displays one of his fall trees. The brown twig tree has been placed in a large salt-glazed crock and decorated with handmade fall ornaments. When the sun sets for the day, the fall tree is ablaze with color and makes the breakfast room feel even more special.

LEFT: A large early bowl with a repair has been filled with small pie pumpkins and placed on the table in the breakfast room.

RIGHT: A pumpkin with a long stem has been placed in an early rye basket to give the top of the apothecary cabinet a seasonal touch.

LEFT: Early dough bowls fill the inside of an early one door cupboard. The inside of the cupboard still maintains its original red paint. BELOW: An early one door cupboard, which boasts its original blue paint, is topped with a collection of small breadboards and a reproduction tin light. A piece of early flax is draped over the cupboard door, while a small white pumpkin is nestled on the top of the cupboard.

OPPOSITE: A brown twig tree has been placed in a large slat-glazed crock and decorated with handmade ornaments. The lights on the tree are white and orange and give the tree an autumnal glow. The top of an early table with its original blue base is the perfect spot to display a single white pumpkin that has been placed in a wooden trencher. The early red hanging cupboard was originally a seed display in a store.

ABOVE: An early apothecary cabinet, which was taken out of an old sewing factory in South Carolina, is topped with two early treen boards, a hogscraper candlestick, and a small rye basket. An early oil portrait hangs above the apothecary.
RIGHT: A small handmade black cat from Arnett's Country Store sits on the ledge of the apothecary.

OPPOSITE: An early sawbuck table sits on an early Oriental rug in the breakfast room. Early mule-eared ladder-back chairs with original green paint surround the table. An early dough bowl filled with pie pumpkins has been placed on the tabletop. The bowl rests on an early Oriental rug remnant that has been used as a table runner.

RIGHT: An early red dry sink occupies the space below a window in the breakfast room.

Reflections of Autumn

Every year when autumn rolls around, Facebook, Instagram, and Pinterest begin to fill with images of the season, and people begin to reminisce about the autumns of their pasts. It seems that most of us agree that autumn is our favorite season. After the long, hot summer, it is easy to see why so many of us look forward to cooler days and nights and being able to wear more than shorts and a t-shirt. As soon as we experience that first burst of fall in the air, our minds begin to reflect on what the season brings and our hearts seem to turn those vibrant autumn colors in preparation for the season.

When I reflect on autumn, my mind is flooded with so many memories. I see myself huddled around a little black-and-white TV at my grandparents' lakehouse watching the *Jerry Lewis Telethon*. I see my family gathering at the same lakehouse to celebrate my mom's birthday. I hear my grandma laugh as she opens a birthday gift from my brothers and me, and I see her eyes fill with tears as she reads the verse in the card. I see brightly colored trees outside my grade school window. I see lines of children dressed in plastic Halloween costumes marching down the street in front of the grade school, and I see bright orange cookies and cupcakes being passed out.

I see my brothers and me piling in the backseat of the car while my mom drives us around town, occasionally stopping at a church member's house. I hear us collectively saying trick-or-treat and being handed a popcorn ball or a gift certificate for free french fries from McDonalds. I feel the excitement of celebrating my own birthday. I can taste the tacos my mom made for my birthday dinner, and I can smell the candles being blown out on my Garfield birthday cake. I can feel the anticipation of looking out the window waiting for my grandma and grandpa to pull into the driveway for Thanksgiving, and I can hear the gentle rustle of newspapers while my aunt looks at the Thanksgiving sale bills. All of these reflections fill my mind, and more importantly my heart, as autumn draws near.

also know that each one of you has autumn reflections that fill your heart and mind each year. As those reflections begin to come to mind, it is easy to long for those simpler times and even to feel a little sad that those days are gone. Even while writing this, I feel a little pang of regret that I did not appreciate those days a little more, but at the same time I realize how blessed I am to have those memories and that as long as I live, those memories will never really be gone. They will live in my heart, and they will reflect in my eyes for many more years to come.

We should learn from our past and remember that even today will be a reflection in our minds tomorrow, so it is up to each one of us to decide what we want our reflections to be. Will we reflect positivity, love, forgiveness, and joy or will we reflect negativity, hatred, unforgiveness, and sadness? Of all the memories we have of autumn, the common thread is love, and after all the years, all the changes, and all the endings, it is love that remains. So let's all make sure that the reflections of our lives are filled with love, and let's all continue to make good memories and never forget the memories we have. I know if we will all do that, the reflections of our lives will be ones that we want to revisit over and over again. Positive reflections of love and family lead to peace, and **PEACE MATTERS.**

"Positivity has no choice but to be reflected back to you."

Bedroom

Over the years, the guest bedroom has evolved. As its evolution has continued, it is rising in the ranks and becoming another one of my favorite spaces. Red is my favorite color, so the different shades of red that this room always make me smile. When autumn arrives, I like to fill the bedroom with folk art and natura pumpkins. One of my favorite aspects of the room is the early linen mattress cover and pillowcase case th are used to spruce up the early red rope bed. I love the simplicity of the bed, and the addition of the early bear holding a pumpkin while leaning against a Halloween pillow made by Bridgett Swindle completes th bed and gives it a vintage autumnal look. The lone wood wall, which has been painted a soothing, dark-gr color, gives the bedroom an earlier appearance and allows one to feel like he has literally stepped back in time.

LEFT: A "double-decker" pumpkin head made by Stacee Droit sits on an early red trunk at the foot of the red rope bed. The early cupboard with a large door is topped with an early green trunk, salt-glazed crock jug, and an early basket.

RIGHT: A stack of early blue and white wool blankets rests on the trunk, while a bittersweet-colored jelly cupboard sits between the two windows in the bedroom.

RIGHT: An Arnett's Country Store
scarecrow stands on top of an early brown
mule chest. BELOW: Three small pumpkins
have been displayed on a mustard-colored
shelf which hangs above a small black
document box that has been topped with
early leather books and a hogscraper
candlestick. BELOW RIGHT: An early
rocking chair sits next to the mule chest.
The shelf contains three gathering baskets
displayed in graduated size and an early
landscape oil painting.

OPPOSITE: An early slant top desk with its original paint has been attached to the wall next to the bed. The misshapen stool serves as the perfect resting spot for a white pumpkin. The desk contains a collection of tiny leather books, a hogscraper candlestick, and small, vintage blocks. An early rectangular sampler hangs above the desk.

RIGHT: An early red rope bed sits in the center of the wood wall in the spare bedroom. An early feather-filled mattress has been used on the bed. The early linen mattress cover serves as a comforter on which to rest the early pillow with linen pillowcase. An early nightshirt and overalls hang near the bed for easy access.

Kids' Room

Who among us does not have wonderful memories of being a kid at Halloween? When decorating the kids' room for autumn, I tried to evoke that childlike feeling. The playfulness of all of the colors in this bedroom draws me in every single time that I walk past it. The room continues to fill up with early toys, and with the addition of the newest bear or pull toy, my heart becomes a little more full. One of my favorite things to do in the kids' room is to use vintage alphabet blocks to spell out words that mean something to me. Three of the words that I create during the fall are joy, autumn, and Ruth. Speaking of my grandma, the early blue box that sits on the trunk at the end of the bed once belonged to her father. My great-grandpa lost a leg and used to sit on the box while he did his gardening. The addition of the box in this room brings my grandma and the stories of her childhood a little closer to mind when I spend time in this room.

An early rocking horse sits atop an early blue pie safe in the kid's room. An early blue child's dress hangs from the door of the pie safe and adds a sense of warmth and softness to the display. Vintage alphabet blocks have been used to spell out the word autumn, and a bright-orange pumpkin sits on the horse to give the room a subtle touch of the season.

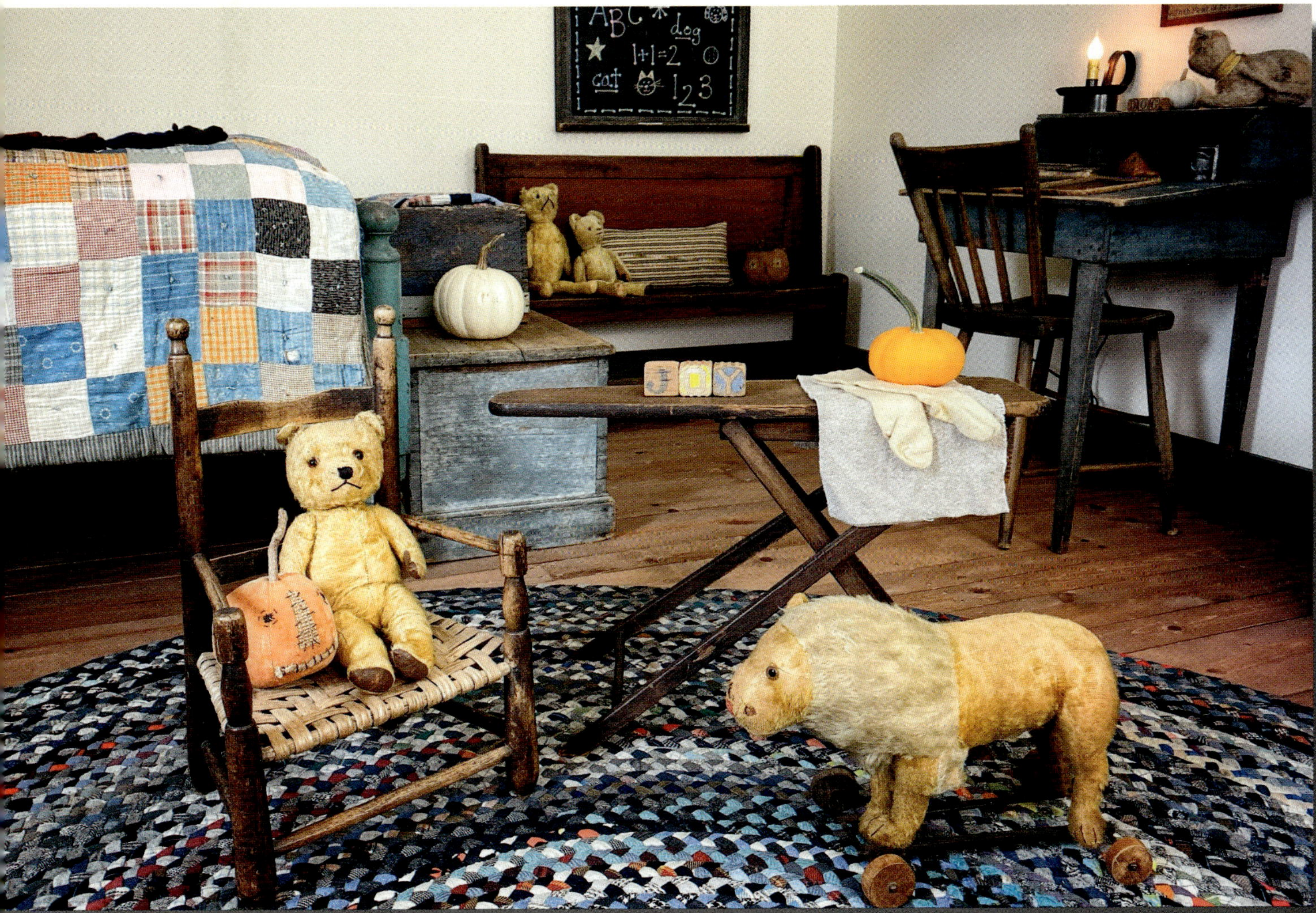

ABOVE: A collection of early bears sits on an early blue bench next to the blue rope bed in the kids' room. An early blue document box, early children's shoes, reproduction tin light, vintage blocks, and books complete the display. A basket full of alphabet blocks sits next to an early Steiff elephant pull toy on the floor in front of the bench. In the foreground, an early bear relaxes in an old child's chair. LEFT: An early blue blanket chest sits at the foot of the bed. The chest has been topped with an early blue box that has been filled with a vintage quilt.

Master Bedroom

The master bedroom is meant to be a place of rest and relaxation. It is meant to be a space where all the troubles of this world seem to fade away and rest can be found. When decorating the master bedroom, I tried to keep the space calming and uncluttered. When decorating the room for autumn, I tried to follow the same philosophy. I added natural pumpkins sparingly to the room and tried to include only small accents of the season. The large, black pencil post bed with a canopy is what the eye is naturally drawn to when entering the room, so I like to use calming blues in the bedding. For autumn, I filled the wooden bowls that sit atop each nightstand with one lone pumpkin. When selecting pumpkins, I like to choose ones with long, misshapen stems. I believe this characteristic gives each pumpkin a unique look. I also chose to use a white pumpkin in one bowl and an orange pumpkin in the other bowl. The two different colors give the nightstands individuality, while still maintaining the uniformity and consistency that I like to incorporate into my decorating.

LEFT: An early mule chest with its original red paint sits between the two windows in the master bedroom. An early document box sits on the top of the chest.

RIGHT: A handmade reproduction sampler in an old Victorian era frame hangs above the chest. The verse on the sampler comes from the book of Ruth.

Whither thou Goest I will Go and where thou Lodgest I will Lodge. ThY PeoPle shall be mY PeoPle and thY God mY God. Ruth 1:16

Olive 1825

ABOVE: A pair of fireside chairs by Johnston Benchworks creates a seating area in the master bedroom. The chairs are separated by an early red table. An oil portrait from the early part of the 20th century hangs above the table.

Conclusion

"I had the strangest dream last night!" If I heard my grandma say that once in her life, I heard her say it a million times. My grandma was a firm believer in dreams, and she truly believed that God communicated with her through her dreams. She developed this belief because of her mother, who had been taught the same thing by her grandmother. My grandma passed the belief in dreams on to my mother who then again passed it on to me. Over the course of approximately 130 years, the belief in the power of dreams and that God uses them to communicate with us had been passed down generation to generation, and it continues with me.

It seemed that anytime a major life event was in store for my grandma, she would have a dream about it. She would have this same dream repeatedly, and she would interpret it as time went on. She truly believed her dreams were powerful conversations with God. I have notebook after notebook of my grandma's writings, and in those notebooks are pages and pages of my grandma writing about her dreams. Those notebooks, as well as the memories of her telling me about those dreams, are a treasure trove of evidence that God does indeed communicate with us, and He will use whatever avenue He can to get a message to us. My grandma was a firm believer in hearing God's voice, and she would often say, "I know it was Him. I recognize His voice." As the years have gone by, I seem to understand her words more and more.

During the bleakness of that autumn of 2014 that I wrote about in the introduction, I held on to the dream I had the morning of my 42nd birthday. I talked about it to Jeff, and I held the dream of living in a saltbox close to my heart, and whenever the road seemed too long or it seemed too impossible to believe, I was reminded of the dream and my heart would feel that peace that the dream had brought to my spirit. As Jeff and I were walking the path that eventually led to finding saltbox bliss, my grandma's journey on this earth was coming to an end, and it was her words of advice and her wisdom that assisted me in completing this house. My grandma's influence is all over this house, and she has touched every single surface in one way or the other.

The miracle of the dream I had on my 42nd birthday came full circle in the latter part of 2017 when the saltbox was nearing completion. We had been waiting for the post office to provide us with the house number of our new address so that we could complete a few unfinished tasks, and finally we got the answer. The number was 1067, and I knew when I heard it that it was a significant number. In fact, while we were waiting to find out the number, I knew it would be significant. When Jeff shared with me the number, I told him it meant something, but I didn't know what. However, I had learned from my grandma that if I were patient, the meaning would be revealed to me. Later that evening while I was preparing for the next day, I was thinking about the number. I knew it had something to do with my grandma, but what? Then it occurred to me. The first number of our new address was 10. The tenth month of the year is October. My grandma was born in October. Then I started thinking about the last two numbers. I started thinking about the year 1967, so I decided to figure out how old my grandma turned in October 1967. When I did the mental math, a wave of amazement and understanding flowed through my body and soul simultaneously. On October 12, 1967, my grandma turned 42, the exact same age I turned the morning that I had the dream about a saltbox with dark gray siding and brilliant red windows. The dream that was the first rung to me climbing out of my pit had been God's way of communicating with me. It had been His way of saying better days are coming and to keep believing in miracles. And as strange as it may sound, God used the address of this house, the saltbox that changed everything, as confirmation that He and my grandma had been guiding Jeff and me every step of the way.

Finding bliss is all about how we approach life, and no one had a better approach to life than my grandma, Ruth Cutsinger. She was a natural-born story teller and teacher, and she taught everyone she met so many valuable lessons about how to live a life that was rooted in faith, hope and love. She led by example, and she wanted her stories, and the stories of all the people she loved, to live on long after she was gone. She felt it was her calling to tell these stories, and she feverishly answered that call all the days of her life. Even now, years after she has gone to heaven, those stories continue to spread and continue to find a new audience. I can almost see her jumping for joy in heaven every time a new person is encouraged by one of her stories or learns a valuable lesson from one of her many struggles. Whenever she would feel like she was not qualified to tell the stories of her life or of her mother's life, she was always reminded of Psalms 78 verses 6-7. The verses read:

> That the generations to come might know them, even the children which should
> be born; who should arise and declare them to their children. That they might set
> their hope in God and not forget the works of God, but keep His commandments.

This scripture encouraged my grandma and has in turn encouraged me. As I once again complete a book about Peace Manor, I stand in amazement of all that has happened. When I think of the miracle of this house, my heart and soul are filled with more thankfulness than I can even describe, and to think it all started from a little dream during the most difficult time in my life. It is like my grandma always said, "God can make good come from any bad situation." If you only remember one thing from this book, I want you to remember that. I want you to remember that no matter how difficult or hopeless your situation may become, God is still in control. I want you to remember that he can build your dreams out of the ashes. I want you to remember that to build anything great sometimes everything has to be knocked down first.

Thank you so much for once again reading my words and looking at my pictures. Your support and interest mean more to me than I can say. Being able to tell my story and the stories of my grandma fill my heart with such peace and as you all know, **PEACE MATTERS**.

Acknowledgments *& Resource Guide*

I would like to thank the following people for helping make this book possible:

Jacob Coy
Ruth Cutsinger
Stacee Droit
Jim Hawkinson
Jim Rapp
Aaron Thomas
Kristine Walden
Andrew Weaver
Darlene Weaver
George Weaver
Jeff Weaver-White
Brian Whittington
Scott Williams

Foyer
Wall Color: Crisp Linen by Sherwin-Williams
Trim Color: Suitable Brown by Sherwin-Williams
Floor Stain Color: Clove Brown by Pittsburgh Paint & Stains
Scarecrow: Arnett's Country Store (arnettscountrystore.com)

Living Room
Wall Color: Crisp Linen by Sherwin-Williams
Trim Color: Carriage Door by Sherwin-Williams
Chandelier: Bill Smokestack by Carriage House Lighting & Tinware (chltin.com)
Sofa: Johnston Benchworks Furniture
Hooked Rug: Betty Zahn
Witch and Black Cat: Arnett's Country Store
Hallows Eve Sampler: Bridgett Swindle
Blanket Crane: Whitehouse Creations (573-421-8028)

Dining Room
Wall Color: Crisp Linen by Sherwin-Williams
Trim Color: Carriage Door by Sherwin-Williams
Chandelier: Bill Smokestack by Carriage House Lighting & Tinware
Floor Stain Color: Clove Brown by Pittsburgh Paint & Stains
Windsor Chairs: Benner's Woodworking (bennerswoodworking.com)
Pumpkin with Witch Hat: Arnett's Country Store

Kitchen:
Wall Color: Crisp Linen by Sherwin-Williams
Trim Color: Carriage Door by Sherwin-Williams
Chandelier: Bill Smokestack by Carriage House Lighting & Tinware
Windsor Bar Stools & Chairs: Benner's Woodworking
Kitchen Cabinets & Countertops: Rapp Cabinets & Wood Works (rappcabinets.com)
Soapstone Sink: Vermont Soapstone Co. (vermontsoapstone.com)

Keeping Room:
Wall Color: Crisp Linen by Sherwin-Williams
Trim Color: Carriage Door by Sherwin-Williams
Chandelier: Bill Smokestack by Carriage House Lighting & Tinware
Floor Stain Color: Clove Brown by Pittsburgh Paint & Stains
Sofas: Johnston Benchworks Furniture
Scarecrow: Arnett's Country Store

Breakfast Room:
Wall Color: Crisp Linen by Sherwin-Williams
Trim Color: Suitable Brown by Sherwin-Williams
Chandelier: Four Arm Whaler by Carriage House Lighting & Tinware
Black Cat: Arnett's Country Store

Bedroom:
Wall Color: Crisp Linen by Sherwin-Williams
Trim Color: Suitable Brown by Sherwin-Williams
Floor Stain Color: Clove Brown by Pittsburgh Paint & Stains
Chandelier: Four Arm Whaler by Carriage House Lighting & Tinware
Doubledecker Pumpkin Head: Arnett's Country Store
Hallows Eve 1783 Pillow: Bridgett Swindle

Kids' Room:
Wall Color: Crisp Linen by Sherwin-Williams
Trim Color: Suitable Brown by Sherwin-Williams
Floor Stain Color: Clove Brown by Pittsburgh Paint & Stains
Chandelier: Four Arm Whaler by Carriage House Lighting & Tinware

Master Bedroom:
Wall Color: Crisp Linen by Sherwin-Williams
Trim Color: Suitable Brown by Sherwin-Williams
Pencil Post Bed: Gary Stott (excelsiorwoodworking.com)
Chandelier: Four Arm Whaler by Carriage House Lighting & Tinware
Fireside Chairs: Johnston Benchworks Furniture
Black Cat in Pumpkin: Arnett's Country Store